LISTENING FOR GOD
THROUGH
EPHESIANS

Lectio Divina Bible Studies

wph
publishing
house

Indianapolis, Indiana

Beacon Hill Press of Kansas City
Kansas City, Missouri

Copyright © 2006 by Wesleyan Publishing House
Published by Wesleyan Publishing House and Beacon Hill Press of Kansas City
Indianapolis, Indiana 46250
Printed in the United States of America

ISBN-13: 978-0-89827-320-5
ISBN-10: 0-89827-320-x

Written by Ken Heer.

ABOUT THE
LECTIO DIVINA
BIBLE STUDIES

ectio divina, Latin for *divine reading,* is the ancient Christian practice of communicating with God through the reading and study of Scripture. Throughout history, great Christian leaders including John Wesley have used and adapted this ancient method of interpreting Scripture. This Bible study builds on this practice, introducing modern readers of the Bible to the time-honored tradition of "listening for God" through His Word. In this series, the traditional *lectio divina* model has been revised and expanded for use in group Bible study. Each session in this study includes the following elements. (Latin equivalents are noted in italics.)

- Summary   A brief overview of the session.
  Epitome

- Silence   A time of quieting oneself prior to
  Silencio   reading the Word.

- Preparation   Focusing the mind on the central
  Praeparatio   theme of the text.

- Reading   Carefully reading a passage of
  Lectio   Scripture.

- Meditation   Exploring the meaning of the Bible
  Meditatio   passage.

- Contemplation   Yielding oneself to God's will.
  Contemplatio

- Prayer   Expressing praise, thanksgiving,
  Oratio   confession, or agreement to God.

- Incarnation   Resolving to act on the message of
  Incarnatio   Scripture.

The Lectio Divina Bible Studies invite readers to slow down, read Scripture, meditate upon it, and prayerfully respond to God's Word.

CONTENTS

INTRODUCTION

In the book of Ephesians, God's children are called to heavenly living in a less-than-heavenly world. God has "raised us up with Christ and seated us with him in heavenly realms" (2:6) and "blessed us in the heavenly realms" (1:3). While we have a new life in Christ and a new relationship with God that is filled with new blessings, we continue to live in our old-world environment—dominated by "the ways of this world" and under the influence of "the spirit who is now at work in those who are disobedient" (2:2).

This book was written to a group of believers in the city of Ephesus whom Paul had helped to come to faith in Christ. The founding of that church is recorded in Acts 16.

Ephesus was a Greek city under Roman occupation. It had a rich, cosmopolitan culture that had been captured by the immorality and idolatries of paganism. It was essential that believers there be assured of their doctrine, their position in Christ, and their defenses against attacks on their faith.

With this need in clear view, the text lifts us into the lofty heights of doctrinal truth and spiritual blessing, and then plunges us into the day-to-day experience of applying that doctrine in the realities of life in this world. It prepares us for the reality of living with the dual positions of being in Christ and in the world.

Paul uses superlative words to describe and define our position in Christ. We find words like: *glorious, incomparable, immeasurable, unsearchable, manifold, surpassing, lavished*—all used in connection with the blessings God has bestowed upon us in heavenly realms so we can live effectively in earthly realms.

As you meditate upon God's Word to believers living in an unbelieving culture, allow Him to help you see the timeless truths needed for you to remain vital in your connection to Christ and vibrant in your witness.

The Apostle Paul wrote this letter that you might be assured of your position in Christ; aware of your privileges, armed against the powers and principalities of this world, and able to live with a bit of heaven on earth.

LIVING IN GOD'S BLESSINGS

Listening for God through Ephesians 1:3–23

SUMMARY

God is the Great Initiator. He begins things in our lives that we are incapable of beginning ourselves. Anything good in our world and in our lives finds its origin and completion in God. He has a good purpose and a good plan for everything and everyone—including you. Life begins and ends with Him.

Grace is God's agent for accomplishing His purpose and plan in human lives. It is the favor of God that is undeserved and unearned: a gift given freely with the only condition that it is received by faith. God enjoys lavishing His grace on those who place their faith in Him.

Because of our sin, we are by nature outside God's saving grace and separated from His spiritual life. Through Christ, though, we can be chosen by God, forgiven of our sins, adopted into His spiritual family, included in His blessings, and guaranteed an eternal inheritance.

God's purpose is that you become His child and enjoy the blessings of life in Christ. Are you ready to step into His blessings?

SILENCE ✝ LISTEN FOR GOD

In silence, acknowledge that you are a child of God through faith in Christ. Listen as the Holy Spirit of God confirms in your spirit that you are His child.

PREPARATION ✝ FOCUS YOUR THOUGHTS

Do you know what it means to be excluded from a group or a benefit enjoyed by others? Conversely, what does it feel like to be chosen?

What do you consider to be the greatest benefit of being chosen to be in God's family?

READING ✝ HEAR THE WORD

Many people consider the study of doctrine to be disinteresting and disconnected from real life. In this section of Scripture, though, Paul presents the doctrine of salvation in terms that meaningfully connect with us. You will encounter some terms that are rich with meaning. Here are a few of them:

Chosen: The Jews were called God's chosen people. In Christ you, too, are one of His chosen.

Adopted: Being adopted into the family of God, with all of its benefits, is a result of being chosen.

Predestined: God had you in mind before you knew Him. In Christ He decided He wanted you to be a part of His eternal family. He is even now at work in your life, encouraging you to respond to His offer of grace.

Forgiven: Only God is able to remove the guilt of your sin and the judgment that is against it. In Christ God frees you from sin's penalty.

Inheritance: Because you have been forgiven and adopted into God's family, you have a guaranteed eternal inheritance—a heavenly home where you will be with God and all other redeemed persons.

With these terms in mind, prayerfully read Ephesians 1:3–23.

MEDITATION † ENGAGE THE WORD

Meditate on Ephesians 1:3–8

Verse 3 says God has blessed us "with every spiritual blessing." In what ways has God blessed you? Verses 4–8 describe
some of the spiritual blessings available in Christ. What meaning does each of these blessings carry in your life?

Verse 4 says it is God's intent that we be "holy and blameless."
What does this mean? How does a person become holy? How
is holiness demonstrated practically in your life?

Read the quote by Keith Drury.
He says the *condition* of holiness
results from the *activity* of sanctification. Where do you find the
word *sanctification* in the
Scriptures? What do you understand it to mean?

> We become holy—
> Christlike—through
> sanctification…Sanc-
> tification is God's Spirit at
> work in my mind, soul,
> spirit, body—my entire life—
> changing and renewing my
> desires, thoughts, interests,
> attitudes, and behaviors.
> —Keith Drury

Are there compartments of your mind, soul, spirit, and body
where you know God is acting presently to sanctify you?

Meditate on Ephesians 1:9–14

These verses indicate that the will of God involves His purpose, plan, and pleasure. What is the meaning of each of these?

Read the Roman proverb in the sidebar. Do you have a good sense of what God's purpose is for your life? Are you accepting

> When the pilot does not know what port he is heading for, no wind is the right wind.
> —Roman Proverb

His plan so the winds that come your way will move you toward the destination God has for you?

Verse 13 says that in Christ you were included. From what had you been excluded? On what basis have you now been included? How would you describe your feelings about being included?

Meditate on Ephesians 1:15–23

In these verses we gain a glimpse inside the heart of Paul and especially into his prayer life. What does he say about his relationship with the people in Ephesus?

When he tells them he remembers them in his prayers, what

specific things does he say he prays for in regard to them? Which of these things would you most like someone to pray for you? Who in your life could become your prayer partner?

Verse 23 speaks of "the fullness of him who fills everything in every way." What do you suppose Paul means by *fullness*? In what ways does God fill everything in every way?

> The river grows larger by its tributaries, but where is the tributary that can enlarge the One out of whom came everything and to whose infinite fullness all creation owes its being?
>
> —A.W. Tozer

A.W. Tozer said the fullness of God refers to His self-sufficiency: He needs nothing to complete Himself, and He is never diminished. Read the Tozer quote in the sidebar. In what ways must you find your sufficiency in Him who alone is fully self-sufficient?

Read the sidebar about St. Theresa's confidence in the ability of God. This is consistent with verse 19, where Paul says the "incomparably great

> St. Theresa once wanted to build an orphanage but she had only three shillings. Someone jeeringly said to her, "What can you do to build an orphanage with only three shillings?" She replied, "Theresa with three shillings, can do nothing, but with three shillings and with God to help there is nothing that Theresa cannot do!"

power" of God is at work on your behalf. How has the power of God been demonstrated recently in your life? When would you have been sunk without His help?

CONTEMPLATION ✝ REFLECT AND YIELD

Is the redemptive purpose of God being fully realized in your life?

How can you trace the plan of God unfolding in your life?

PRAYER ✝ RESPOND TO GOD

Paul said God chose you to be the beneficiary of His spiritual blessings and to "sit with Christ in heavenly realms." Are you enjoying the blessings that are promised you as a child of God?

Pray now that all of the spiritual blessings of Christ may be fully released and realized in you.

INCARNATION ✝ LIVE THE WORD

Grace is the favor of God offered freely to you. For a gift to be possessed, it must be accepted. God has taken the initiative to offer you a great plan for your life. It is now up to you to accept that plan and act on it—to live in the blessings He made possible.

How will your life be different this week in light of the blessings you have in Christ?

LIVING A TRANSFORMED LIFE

Listening for God through Ephesians 2:1–22

SUMMARY

The best way to see the changes that have occurred in a person or place is to have before and after pictures—a comparison of the present with the past. In matters of faith it is much the same. The grace of God, extended in Christ and activated through the presence and power of the Holy Spirit, transforms us so that we are not what we once were.

Some changes that have happened in your life may be obvious to you and to those who know you. These outward, visible changes are the result of a transformation in the kind of person you are now on the inside—your nature has been changed.

Paul says God has not only forgiven you and adopted you into His forever family, but He has transformed (and will continue to transform) your nature as He constructs a temple for His Spirit inside you.

SILENCE ✝ LISTEN FOR GOD

The Spirit of God dwells within you. Listen as He speaks peace and calm into your spirit.

PREPARATION ✝ FOCUS YOUR THOUGHTS

What has changed about you since you accepted Christ? Do you like the person you have become?

If you could change something else about yourself, what would it be?

READING ✝ HEAR THE WORD

Paul is writing to first-generation believers—people who came to Christ out of paganism. Ephesus was a place where many different religions converged and were often intermingled with idolatry, witchcraft, and immorality.

It is impossible to embrace Christ while continuing to embrace pagan practices. When people come to Christ, their way of living must change. But practices can become habits that are hard to change. Something fundamental to the nature of a person must be changed for habitual behavior to be changed.

Read Ephesians 2:1–22. As you do, note how these verses give a picture of what you used to be and how God has changed you so you are capable of living a transformed life.

MEDITATION ✝ ENGAGE THE WORD

Meditate on Ephesians 2:1–3

Paul describes your pre-Christian life as being dead in transgressions and sins. In what ways were you dead before you came to Christ?

The text also says the "ways of this world" influence the way people live. What are these ways, and how do they impact behavior?

Read the quote from comedian Fred Allen. Why is that way of living both dangerous and displeasing to God?

> Most of us spend the first six days of each week sowing wild oats; then we go to church on Sunday and pray for a crop failure.
>
> —Fred Allen

Paul indicates that the way we used to live was influenced by our sins, the ways of the world, the evil spirit that is at work, and our sinful nature. He says our sinful nature has cravings, desires, and thoughts that make up a nature in us that is displeasing to God. In what areas of your own life have you felt the displeasure of God?

Meditate on Ephesians 2:4–10

Our after picture is much better to look at than our before picture. It is made possible because of God's love, mercy, and grace. How would you describe the meaning of each of these transformational agents of God?

We were "dead in transgressions," now we are "alive with Christ." How would you describe what it is like to be alive with Christ?

When we are saved, God raises us up. What does it mean to you that God has raised you up?

Grace is the most optimistic thing in the world. It says that anyone can be changed. It offers hope for this life and the one to come. There is nothing we are or can do to deserve salvation—it is a gift of grace. What are some ways people try to earn salvation? On what basis might people think they deserve salvation? Why is this contrary to what God's Word says?

Verse 10 says you are now the special object of God's creation. He is working on you. He is preparing you for something good. In what areas of your life are you conscious that God has been at work? What are some good works that you sense God is preparing you to do?

Read the sidebar quote of William Jordan. Who are the people most influenced by your transformed life? Why is this the case?

> Into the hands of every individual is given a marvelous power for good or evil—the silent, unconscious, unseen influence of his life.
>
> —William George Jordan

Meditate on Ephesians 2:11–20

Circumcision was an outward, physical act to which male Jews submitted as a sign of their identification with Jehovah God. By birth Gentiles were uncircumcised outsiders—separated foreigners to God's covenant with Israel. What was God's purpose in having a chosen people? How was this outward sign indicative of an inner commitment?

Verse 12 says we were once "without God" and "without hope." Who are some people you know who live without God and without hope? In what ways do they demonstrate this reality?

In verse 12 Paul asks the Ephesian believers to remember their former lives. While there may be things of our past that we are ashamed of and would just as soon forget, it may be helpful to occasionally remember how life used to be when we were separated and excluded. Having remembered how it used to be, what feelings do you now have about being included and having hope?

Verse 13 says it is through the blood of Christ that we have been included within God's covenant and blessing. Verse 16 says the cross has been the agent of reconciling everyone, regardless of nationality, to God. Why was the death of Christ necessary?

Verse 18 says that through Christ we have "access to the Father." What does this mean? How are you taking advantage of this privilege?

Meditate on Ephesians 2:21–22

These verses have both corporate and individual meaning. The people of God as a community come together as a "holy temple in the Lord." God has chosen to dwell with and demonstrate His presence through the Church—the community of believers. How have you witnessed the presence and power of God within your church?

Read the quote from Bill Bright. Compare it to verse 22 where Paul says the Spirit of God seeks to dwell in you as a person. There is some building going on inside you so you can be a fit dwelling place for God. Where has He had to do some demolition? What improvements has He made since He has come to live inside you?

> To be filled with the Holy Spirit is to be filled with Christ...If I am controlled and empowered by Christ, He will be walking around in my body, living His resurrection life in and through me.
>
> —Bill Bright

CONTEMPLATION ✝ REFLECT AND YIELD

Are you comfortable with the realization that you are a temple for God to live in? Are there specific areas of your life that you have had difficulty yielding to the transforming work of God?

What might be different in your life if you were "filled with the Spirit"?

PRAYER ✝ RESPOND TO GOD

The grace of God through Christ changes our relationship and standing with God as it changes the kind of people we are. How has grace changed you? Where is God at work in you right now?

Pray silently, thanking God for including you in His family and asking Him to show you any area of your life that needs to be changed.

INCARNATION ✝ LIVE THE WORD

We are witnesses to the changes God has brought into our lives through our word and work—what we say and what we do. Make a list of three people to whom you can tell your before-and-after story during the next two weeks.

What is one area of pressure you experience from the "ways of this world"? Decide today how you are going to react when you face that pressure again.

LIVING IN THE PURPOSE AND POWER OF GOD

Listening for God through Ephesians 3:1~21

SUMMARY

God has a purpose for the world and for your life. He has a plan that He is working out that will fulfill His purpose. Some moments it may appear as if God is not in control, but He has an intent, a purpose, and a plan that are demonstrated in the flow of history. It is in knowing the purpose God has for you and experiencing the power of God within you that you discover how to experience and maintain an earth-bound life with a bit of heaven in it. Your personal courage and conviction will grow out of the belief that you are being and doing what God intends.

Paul had a good grip on his purpose in life. His purpose was inextricably intertwined with God's purpose. His work in the world was a part of God's plan.

Yet having a purpose and a plan is not enough. You must have the power to carry out your purpose and plan, or they are only empty rhetoric and unrealistic dreams. God not only has power beyond your imagination to carry out His purpose and plan, but that power is at work in you to help fulfill your life's purpose and engage yourself effectively in God's plan.

SILENCE ✝ LISTEN FOR GOD

What is your favorite descriptive term for Jesus? Speak that term in your mind and listen as God reminds you of times when that name for Jesus has had special meaning to you.

PREPARATION ✝ FOCUS YOUR THOUGHTS

What is God up to in the world? What do you believe to be His purpose for your life? If God could do something in your life that you are incapable of doing yourself, what do you think it might be?

READING ✝ HEAR THE WORD

The Apostle Paul was on a mission from God to make plain to everyone God's purpose for humankind. At times it might have appeared to be a mystery as to what God was up to. The mission of Paul was to proclaim that the gospel—the good news—was for everyone, Jew or Gentile. His purpose was to be sure others understood the purpose of God and lived within the blessings of His grace.

Paul was clear in this purpose. In this passage he refers to himself as "the prisoner of Christ" and "a servant of the gospel." Both *prisoner* and *servant* might be considered demeaning and restrictive. Did Paul behave as if either were true?

Another of Paul's wonderful prayers is recorded in this passage. He prays that the power of God would be experienced in the lives of these believers so they would be strengthened in their "inner being." Many people who have the power of physique, position, and possessions ultimately fall and fail in life because they are weak on the inside.

Consider these thoughts as you read Ephesians 3:1–21.

MEDITATION ✝ ENGAGE THE WORD

Meditate on Ephesians 3:1–6

Paul had a clear sense that he was living out a mission assignment from God. What brought him to this conviction?

The purpose of Paul's life included bringing a message and blessing to others. Who can you identify in your life who has had a mission of bringing grace, hope, and blessing to you? Do you view your purpose to include a similar mission?

Read the sidebar explanation by Ray Stedman of the mystery mentioned by Paul. Who around you is in desperate need of knowing God's "sacred secrets"?

> The "mysteries" are the sacred secrets that God knows about life, which men desperately need to know.
>
> —Ray Stedman

What is your responsibility for giving insights into the mystery of the gospel to those who need to know?

Meditate on Ephesians 3:7–12

Paul viewed himself to be the least-likely, least-deserving person to be called by God to such an important purpose. But because of grace and the transforming, enabling power of God, he fulfilled his purpose. When have you felt inadequate and less than the least? How has God helped you carry out His plan for you despite your weaknesses and inadequacies?

Read the sidebar quote by Rick Warren. God is the source of our purpose. What He has in mind for you, He has the power to make happen. Do you have the conviction that regardless of your inadequacies and your circumstances, God is working in you and through you to accomplish His purpose?

A part of God's plan is that you have access to His presence, as well as His power. He wants

> The purpose of your life is far greater than your own personal fulfillment, your peace of mind, or even your happiness. It's far greater than your family, your career, or even your wildest dreams and ambitions. If you want to know why you were placed on this planet, you must begin with God. You were born by His purpose and for His purpose.
>
> —Rick Warren

you to approach Him with freedom and confidence. How might this have been a new idea to the readers of this letter? How do we fellowship with an awesome and holy God, while we are wretched sinners?

Meditate on Ephesians 3:13–21

Prayer was a vital part of Paul's relationship with God and of his care about the needs of his friends. He was experiencing suffering, but his prayer for others reflected his reliance upon God for his own adequacy, as well as theirs. Recall times when you've been in your own difficult times, but you carried others to God in prayer. How did praying for others affect you during those times?

Read the sidebar quote from Sherwood Eddy. Can you say that you live with "spiritual power"? If not, how can you?

> We readily admit that Jesus and all the genuine saints throughout history had spiritual power and that they had a deep prayer life. We believe that there must be some connection between their power and their life of prayer.
> —Sherwood Eddy

Verse 16 indicates that our greatest need is for strength in our "inner being." What do you understand this to mean? What is the source of this strengthening?

The words *dwell, rooted,* and *established* in verse 17 speak of permanence and stability. What connection is there between these words as they appear in this passage?

Grasping the dimensions of the love of Christ is a major focus of this prayer. How wide is the love of Christ? How long? How high? How deep? What have you come to understand about this love that exceeds understanding?

Living with a bit of heaven on earth is possible as you live within the purpose, plan, and power of God. What does Paul say regarding God's ability to accomplish this in verse 20?

CONTEMPLATION ✝ REFLECT AND YIELD

Do you understand the purpose God has for you? How are you living out that purpose? Are you ready to follow God's purpose wherever it may take you and do whatever it may call you to do?

PRAYER ✝ RESPOND TO GOD

Read the sidebar statement about prayer. Tell God about your inadequacies, fears, and questions. Experience His mercy and grace flowing into your spirit. He is at work within you and is able to do more than you could ask or imagine. Experience His love and His fullness.

> Our prayer and God's mercy are like two buckets in a well; while the one ascends the other descends.
>
> —Mark Hopkins

INCARNATION ✝ LIVE THE WORD

God wants each of us to be servants of the gospel, helping to spread the word about what He is up to in the world. How can you share the good news at your work this week? Is there a person God brings to your mind who needs to hear the gospel?

LIVING IN A LOVING, GROWING COMMUNITY

Listening for God through Ephesians 4:1–16

SUMMARY

Christians do not try to make it in the world on their own. They come to Christ one person at a time. But from that moment they are a part of a larger community—part of a family. You can find that family of faith anywhere you go in the world. Believers are bound together with common faith, common life, common values, and common purpose.

The family of God takes the shape of a local church community. The church was God's invention for the spiritual stability and growth of His people. It is within the church community that you celebrate your oneness with Christ, you are gifted for service, and you receive the nurture and discipline necessary to mature spiritually.

Living so you experience a bit of heaven on earth will be enhanced through the fellowship, encouragement, and challenge to your spiritual maturity that results from being a part of a local church family.

SILENCE ✝ LISTEN FOR GOD

Breathe a prayer to God, thanking Him for your spiritual family. Listen as He brings to mind the people who have contributed to your salvation and spiritual growth.

PREPARATION ✝ FOCUS YOUR THOUGHTS

What one special time jumps into your mind as a time that your church really supported you and demonstrated Christ's love to you? What is the present status of your relationship with a local church family?

If there is one thing you could do within the church that would help others grow, what would it be?

READING ✝ HEAR THE WORD

Paul has laid the foundation of doctrinal truths and spiritual blessings upon which the readers' faith has been built. He now turns his attention to the importance of relationships within the community of people who have accepted Christ. He tells them about the common things that are bonds between them.

He tells them God has selected persons for leadership within the church and has gifted them to enable all members of the community to serve each other and to serve God in the world. He tells them the church is to be a loving community where people are motivated to grow into spiritual maturity.

With these truths in mind, read Ephesians 4:1–16.

MEDITATION ✝ ENGAGE THE WORD

Meditate on Ephesians 4:1–6

Paul is writing from a Roman prison. However, in none of his writings does he indicate that prison has defeated him or stripped him of his ability to carry out the purpose of his life. In fact, in verse 1 he says he is a "prisoner for the Lord." He is not a prisoner of Rome, but a prisoner for the Lord. What does he mean by this? How could this perspective modify his mood and mission?

Believers have received a calling of which they are to live worthy. What is this calling, and how does a person live up to it?

Read the quote from *Brotherhood Journal*.. Who might be in your Christian family with whom you do not see eye to eye but with whom you are able to walk arm in arm?

> Christians may not see eye to eye, but they can walk arm in arm.
> —Brotherhood Journal

One of the evidences of God's work in people is how they feel toward, and get along with, each other. What virtues characterize Christian community life in verses 2 and 3? How are you contributing to the unity of the church?

The unity of the church finds its origin in the oneness of God and His salvation plan. Read the statement of J.I. Packer regarding the mystery of the Trinity. It is difficult for us to wrap our minds around the possibility of three distinct persons of one essential nature. Yet this doctrinal truth is at the heart of our faith. Sometimes it is just as difficult for us to wrap our arms around

> Here are two mysteries for the price of one—the plurality of persons within the unity of God, and the union of Godhead and manhood in the person of Jesus.
> —J.I. Packer

people who are different and difficult, yet this is at the heart of our faith community. Unity is an expression of the presence and power of God. Where He is, there is unity. How can you begin to express unity in a new way in your church community?

Meditate on Ephesians 4:7–11

God's grace is offered to everyone as a means of salvation. This grace is also at work in every person who is in Christ, transforming them and preparing them for the purpose God has for them. Grace comes in the shape of gifts—talents, spiritual abilities, opportunities, and positions. Paul identified several specific leadership positions for which persons had been gifted—apostles, prophets, evangelists, and pastors/teachers. What do you understand these different positions to be? Are there modern counterparts to these positions? In what ways has God gifted you for service within the church?

Meditate on Ephesians 4:12–16

According to verse 12, the purpose for the functioning of those with leadership gifts is "to prepare God's people for works of service." Is this your view of the purpose of leaders in your church—to prepare *you* for service? Why do people often think those hired to be leaders are the ones responsible to do the work of the church?

The huge redwood trees in California are the tallest trees in the world and some are over 2,500 years old. They have a shallow system of roots, but their roots all intertwine. They are locked to each other, and do not stand alone, for all the trees support and protect each other. What application of this fact can you make to the nature and function of the church?

God's purpose is that all of His children are engaged in service so the "body of Christ may be built up" and "become mature." How does engagement in service contribute to growth and maturity?

In verse 12 the church is referred to as the "body of Christ." What other images are used in the Scripture to portray the nature and function of the church? Which communicates most meaningfully to you?

What are the indicators of immaturity as expressed in verse 14? What are the indicators of maturity as expressed in verses 15–16?

Do you agree with the statement in the sidebar about the indispensable place of the church in your life? What results when

He cannot have God for his Father who refuses to have the church for his mother.

—St. Augustine

Christians neglect a strong attachment to a church where they can experience meaningful, loving relationships?

Living with a bit of heaven on earth is dependant upon being a part of a loving, growing community of believers. Is that how you would describe your church family? What contribution are you making to help make your church a place where people are loved and where they can mature in their Christian faith?

Read Jane Howard's statement in the sidebar. Does this apply to a universal need for the church? Is your need for the church being adequately met? Is the need of others being met by what you contribute to the family of God?

> Call it a clan, call it a network, call it a tribe, call it a family. Whatever you call it, whoever you are, you need one.
>
> —Jane Howard

CONTEMPLATION ♰ REFLECT AND YIELD

How has God gifted you for serving in and through the church? What area of ministry in your church is presently needing help? If God opens an opportunity for you to serve in that area would you be willing to accept it?

PRAYER ✝ RESPOND TO GOD

God has gifted people to give leadership to your church. Do you regularly support them with prayer, respect, and affirmation?

Pray that God will strengthen your church by blessing your leaders and by calling workers who are willing to get engaged in service. Listen for His promptings for how you can serve.

INCARNATION ✝ LIVE THE WORD

Make a list of the characteristics you think should exist in a mature Christian. On a scale of one to five—five being highest—rate yourself on each of the characteristics. What can you begin today that will stimulate spiritual growth in the area in which you need it most?

LIVING A HOLY LIFE

Listening for God through Ephesians 4:17–32

SUMMARY

God calls us to Himself so we can be transformed and live a new life that has Jesus Christ as its pattern. He calls us so that He can accomplish His purposes for us as we cooperate with Him.

One of those purposes, which Paul identified back in chapter 1, is that we be "holy and blameless." Holy living involves how we think, how we express our attitudes, how we speak, and how we behave toward others. There is no part of our life that should remain outside of God's cleansing, transforming work. This holy living requires empowerment by God's Spirit alongside full commitment on our part. God will not violate the free expression of our choice. We have to exercise our decision to put our faith in His forgiving and cleansing power.

The goal of your life should be to become more and more like Jesus. He was kind, compassionate, and forgiving. When you live like Him, you help bring these gifts to others.

SILENCE   LISTEN FOR GOD

Heaven is filled with song as its residents sing to God: Holy, holy, holy! Say those words to God, and listen as He fills your spirit with the peaceful sounds of heaven.

PREPARATION   FOCUS YOUR THOUGHTS

Can you recall a time recently when you were made aware that the way you think and behave is radically different than those in the non-Christian world? How did you react to this difference? Did it make you feel different and odd, or did it affirm your commitment to Christ and cause you to feel encouraged?

Are you happy with the changes God is bringing to your life? Is there a particular area in which you know you need more changing?

Lectio READING HEAR THE WORD

As difficult as it may be sometimes, when we become follow-
ers of Christ we are to be changed people who live differently
than we did before. In fact, God asks that we be holy, as He is
holy. This requires radical changes in us.

Every change we need may not be realized over night, but we need
to commit ourselves to becoming individuals who reflect the work
of God that is going on within us as He makes us Christ-like.

Look for the characteristics Paul gives for those he calls Gentiles.
Do any of these characteristics describe you before you became a
Christian? Do they describe any of the people you see around
you? What is to be your response to your "former way of life"?
What characterizes your new self? Are the ethical and relational
expectations of a new life recognizable in your behavior?

Consider those questions as you read Ephesians 4:17–32.

Meditatio MEDITATION ENGAGE THE WORD

Meditate on Ephesians 4:17–19

Our behavior grows out of how we think and how we view our
world. Gentiles, or unbelievers, are characterized as being
futile in their thinking. What does Paul mean by this? In what
way is the thinking of unbelievers futile?

Read the Oswald Sanders quote. How are his comments consistent with verse 18, which speaks of darkened understanding, ignorance, and hardening of the heart? How is this reflected in the thinking of an unbeliever?

> The mind of man is the battleground on which every moral and spiritual battle is fought.
> —J. Oswald Sanders

Meditate on Ephesians 4:20–24

Most of us are indebted to someone for telling (teaching) us about Jesus. Who have been the great teachers in your life who have both taught you about Jesus and shown you what it means to follow Him?

Verse 22 says we are to put off our old self. What do you understand that to mean? How do you do it?

Verse 23 says we are to have a new attitude and a new mind. How has your way of thinking and your attitude toward life changed since you have become a new creature in Christ?

Read the sidebar about Mahatma Gandhi. We are to become new persons who are to live like Jesus and are created to be like God. He is characterized as being righteous and holy. What do you understand this to mean? Are you righteous and holy? How can you put on a new self that is righteous and holy?

Missionary E. Stanley Jones once asked Mahatma Gandhi how Christianity could be more acceptable in India. His reply was, "I would suggest, first, that all of you Christians…begin to live more like Jesus."

Meditate on Ephesians 4:25–28

Holy living involves how we relate to others. It is as basic as being honest and truthful.

Read the quote from *The Baptist Beacon*. At some point in most people's lives, they have a problem with anger. Paul says when we are angry we should not sin. What does he mean by this? Do you suppose it has something to do with the acid effect of anger?

Anger is an acid that can do more harm to the vessel in which it is stored than to anything on which it is poured.
    –The Baptist Beacon

According to verses 26–27, what is a Christian's responsibility regarding anger? How can expressing anger give the devil a foothold?

Likewise, Paul reminds us in verse 28 that Christians should be engaged in honest labor. Not only should this result in doing beneficial things for others, but also in gaining resources that can be shared with those who are needy. How does this differ from the work motives of many people?

Meditate on Ephesians 4:29–32

As he continues to bring up outward evidences of the new life, Paul reminds us of the power words have to hurt or help others. What kind of talk would you consider to be unwholesome? Conversely, how can the words you speak build up other people?

Verse 30 says we should not grieve the Holy Spirit. What does this mean? How can a person grieve the Holy Spirit?

Bitterness, rage, anger, brawling, slander, and malice are inconsistent with holy living. Have you ever struggled with any of these?

These verses closely connect our relationship with God and our relationship with others—one affects the other. In what ways should your relationship with God affect your relationship with others? Why would your relationship with others affect your relationship with God?

Persons who are living a holy life should demonstrate kindness and compassion toward others. This may involve forgiving those who wrong you, which is to be done as freely and completely as God has forgiven you. Read the quote from Hannah More. Do you agree with her statement? Why or why not?

> A Christian will find it cheaper to pardon than to resent. Forgiveness saves the expense of anger, the cost of hatred, the waste of spirits.
>
> —Hannah More

Why is it hard to forgive some people? Are there persons in your life toward whom you find it difficult to be kind and compassionate? Are there persons you have difficulty forgiving?

CONTEMPLATION   REFLECT AND YIELD

What kind of residue of your life before Christ still exists? Are you willing to let God expose things in you with which He is not pleased? Have you fully consecrated as much as you understand about yourself to God?

PRAYER   RESPOND TO GOD

Salvation is more than being forgiven for your sins. It is being freed from the power sin had over your attitudes and behavior. How has sin's control over you changed since you became a Christian?

Pray and ask God to show you things in your life He wants to cleanse you from, so He can more completely fill you with His Spirit.

INCARNATION   LIVE THE WORD

Jesus said the great commandment was to love God with our entire being and to love others as ourselves. Holy living is relational—involving God and others. It requires us to be kind, compassionate, and forgiving—just like Jesus. Is there anyone who needs your forgiveness? What will you do about it today?

LIVING IN LOVE
AND LIGHT

Listening for God through Ephesians 5:1~20

SUMMARY

We are most like God when we love others. There are
several types of love mentioned in Scripture—each
using a different word in the language of the New Testament.
There is a word that means family love—of a parent for a
child. There is a word that means physical, sensual love. There
is a word that means friendship love—the bond that exists
between people who like to be together. None of these words
adequately defines the love God has for us and the love He
wants us to have for each other. So a new word appears in the
New Testament. This word describes love like God's that
caused Him to give His Son for our salvation. That's the kind
of love He wants to give us for others.

In another vivid image Paul tells us to live in the light. In Scripture, the light is truth that makes clear the difference between good and evil. It is the Holy Spirit exposing the truth about a matter. We are to bring everything to the light of the Scriptures and the Spirit to test its rightness.

The images of love and light can bring us to a fresher understanding of the life God wants us to experience on earth.

SILENCE † LISTEN FOR GOD

Thank God for His Word—the Holy Scriptures. As His Holy Spirit accompanies your reading of His Word, listen as He brings to your mind verses you have memorized or previously read.

PREPARATION † FOCUS YOUR THOUGHTS

Whom do you admire, and how would you like to be like them?

Have people told you that you look like or have some of the characteristics of other members of your family? How does that make you feel?

READING ✝ HEAR THE WORD

Children carry family traits and often imitate the attitudes and behaviors of their parents. They learn to respond to life through the closeness of their relationships. In the same way, by choice and by close relationship, true children of God imitate their Father.

What are some of the traits of our Father that we can emulate? Looking to Christ as our example, we see first a pattern for living a life of love. Verse 2 says love caused Him to give Himself up for us. For many people, love is a means of satisfying emotional needs and gratifying self-centered desires. That leads to the perversion and abuse of love. Following Jesus' example Christians are conscious of how they relate to others.

Christians follow Christ's example by giving up a life that is dominated by the ways of the world and by sinful desires. They live under the powerful influence of the Holy Spirit, whom they have allowed to fill them.

Read Ephesians 5:1–20, and allow these verses to cause you to consider how you can live in the light.

Meditatio

MEDITATION ✝ ENGAGE THE WORD

Meditate on Ephesians 5:1–2

As St. Bernard of Clairvaux says, children are deeply influenced by the people they view to be impor-

> What we love we shall grow to resemble.
> —St. Bernard of Clairvaux

tant. They often will consciously imitate them. They may even unconsciously pattern themselves after these persons, repeating observed behaviors and attitudes. Children of God are to imitate God, consciously choosing to have their behavior and attitudes shaped by Him. How are you imitating your Heavenly Father?

As Henry Ward Beecher states in the sidebar, the love and sacrifice of Christ is to be our pattern. In what way does your life of love demonstrate itself sacrificially?

> We never know how much one loves till we know how much he is willing to endure and suffer for us; and it is the suffering element that measures love.
> —Henry Ward Beecher

The love of Christ was like sweet-smelling perfume to God. Whom do you know who lives such a loving, sacrificial life that wherever they go, it is as if they leave a sweet fragrance behind?

Meditate on Ephesians 5:3–7

The influence of some people should be avoided. Are there people you have learned are a bad influence on you? How have your friendships changed since you became a Christian?

Read the sidebar definition of sin by Walter Carson. Our nature is to distort and pervert the creation of God. How might sexual immorality, impurity, and greed be cheap imitations and perversions of love? Verse 3 says these

> *Sin is twisting and distorting out of its proper shape a human personality which God designed to be a thing of beauty and joy forever.*
>
> —Walter Carson

are improper for God's holy people. How do Christians come to know what is proper and improper?

Paul says out-of-place speaking includes obscenity, foolish talk, and coarse joking. How would you describe the meaning of each of these? What adjectives would you use to characterize your speech?

Verse 5 says immoral, impure, and greedy people are idolaters. How is this so?

The love of God is a major focus of the book of Ephesians. But on a couple of occasions, like in verse 6, Paul speaks of the wrath of God. How do you reconcile the love of God with the wrath of God? Can He be a loving God and also send His wrath upon people—even cut them off from an eternal inheritance?

Meditate on Ephesians 5:8–14

Verse 8 contrasts our life before Christ with our life after Christ as being as different as darkness and light. Earlier Paul said our life without Christ was death. Now he says it was darkness. How is life without Christ like living in darkness?

We are to live as children of light. What do you understand this to mean? How do we live in the light?

Read the sidebar statement about conscience by Tryon Edwards. Are you making your conscience a reliable guide?

> Conscience is merely our own judgment of the right or wrong of our actions, and so can never be a safe guide unless enlightened by the word of God.
>
> —Tryon Edwards

Most people try to hide things in their lives that they know are wrong or that they know should cause them to feel ashamed. Have you ever tried to cover up a wrong and then had it discovered by someone? How did it make you feel? Why is it dangerous and unhealthy to try to cover up wrongs?

Light exposes secret things and makes things visible. Where do believers go to find the light that exposes potential problems in their lives?

Living with goodness, righteousness, and truth frees a person from the fear of having something discovered that might be embarrassing. In what areas of your life are you proving that you have nothing to hide?

Meditate on Ephesians 5:15–20

Christianity is not just a matter of belief. It is also a matter of behavior. Christians live carefully and wisely. What does that mean in practical terms?

Verse 17 says we are to "understand what the Lord's will is." People often struggle with God's will, either because they don't know what it is or they know and are resisting it. Within the context of these verses, what can you understand about God's will for you?

How does the quote from Paul Little help you put verse 17 into a clear light?

Has it ever struck you that the vast majority of the will of God for your life has already been revealed in the Bible?

—Paul Little

Paul encourages the readers to be "filled with the Spirit." What do you understand this to mean? How does a person become filled with the Spirit?

Living in love and light brings joy to a person's spirit. This joy escapes the believer's spirit in the form of uplifting speech and spiritual music. Christians love to sing. The music of their mouths comes from the music in their hearts.

The book of Acts records that Paul and Silas sang songs at midnight when in prison. Scripture says that when Jesus and the disciples left the upper room, and Jesus headed toward the agony of Gethsemane and of Calvary, He led them in singing a song. Has God put a song in your heart that keeps your spirit warm even when the cold winds of adversity are blowing?

CONTEMPLATION ✟ REFLECT AND YIELD

Some things have been made clear in the Scriptures as not being compatible with the Christian life. However, not everything in our world is black and white. Christians need to be discerning and able to find out what pleases God and what doesn't. Are there convictions you have developed based on your sense of what pleases God? Are you willing for God to show you areas where you need to be careful?

PRAYER ✟ RESPOND TO GOD

We are asked to live in love and light. We are to love sacrificially. We are to live carefully and wisely. We are to be filled with the Spirit and have a song in our hearts. Ask God to help these traits and actions become a reality in your life today. Let His Spirit occupy all of your being and compose the music of heaven in your heart.

INCARNATION ✟ LIVE THE WORD

If Scripture and the Spirit are sources of light, what do you need to do to live in the light? Is there a person or a small group with whom you can develop a relationship of accountability as a means of helping you live carefully in light and love?

LIVING IN LOVING RELATIONSHIPS

Listening for God through Ephesians 5:21–6:9

SUMMARY

The healthy Christian life that honors God will include healthy, loving relationships—particularly at home and at work. Healthy relationships must have a bit of submission in them—the willingness to surrender some of each person's will and rights to that of the other person. Yet many people could not describe their home lives in these terms. Their experience is more like poor relationships that suck the joy out of life and heaven out of our spirit.

In the home, marriage is to be a reflection of Christ's love for the church, filled with submissive, self-sacrificing love and respect. Healthy families also include children who obey and honor their parents, and parents who do not exasperate their children.

In the workplace similar principles apply. Workers have a responsibility to work and witness as if they were doing it for Christ, and employers have a responsibility to understand that they answer to God for the way they treat their workers.

SILENCE ✝ LISTEN FOR GOD

Tell God you love Him. Listen as He affirms His love to you.

PREPARATION ✝ FOCUS YOUR THOUGHTS

How does your family build memory moments? What great family moment comes to mind right now?

If you could fix one thing in your family, what would it be?

READING ✝ HEAR THE WORD

The first word in this section of Scripture is a hard one for some people to accept, and harder to put into practice— *submit*. It means to voluntarily yield to the power or authority of another. If two people submit to each other, it means that there will be mutual respect, cooperation, and collaboration. There will be no abuse or manipulation.

The marriage relationship is modeled after Christ's love for the church. Christ's love for the church is to be a model of how a husband should love his wife. Wives are asked to submit to their husbands, but this does not give husbands control rights over their wives because they are also to be submissive, "out of reverence for Christ."

Other words like *love, obey, honor, respect,* and *serve* are found throughout this instruction about relationships. The focus of a Christian in relationship is not upon self, but upon others.

The principle of God's way is that when you invest yourself in others—family, friends, and co-workers—you'll experience the most joy.

Read Ephesians 5:21–6:9, looking for evidence of these truths.

MEDITATION ✝ ENGAGE THE WORD

Meditate on Ephesians 5:21–33

Submission is a choice—a willful decision to yield your rights to another. Why is that hard for most people to do?

The basis for our submission to others is reverence for Christ. What connection does reverence for Christ have with our relationship to others?

Read the statement by Donald Kauffman. Do you agree with this perspective on marriage? What is the difference between a contract and a covenant?

A good marriage is not a contract between two persons but a sacred covenant between three. Too often Christ is never invited to the wedding and finds no room in the home.

–Donald Kauffman

Wives are to submit to their husbands "as to the Lord," and husbands are to love their wives "as Christ loved." How does this moderate the fear of control and domination?

The goal of Christ's love for the church is revealed in verses 26–27. Within that is the goal that the church be holy and blameless—the same goal for individuals that was mentioned in chapter 1. How can the church, as a collection of individuals in a wide range of spiritual development, be holy and blameless?

Meditate on Ephesians 6:1–4

Like *submit, obey* may be considered demeaning or restrictive. There can be something in the human spirit that resists both. What is right about children obeying their parents?

Do you agree with the statement in the sidebar made by the dying father? Why or why not?

A dying Christian father said to his wife, "See that you bring the children up to honor and obey you, for if they don't obey you when they are young, they won't obey God when they are older."

Verse 2 says honoring parents "is the first commandment with a promise." What is meant by this? What is the promise?

Fathers are specifically mentioned in verse 4, but mothers can be included as well. Parents are not to exasperate their children. In what ways might parents exasperate their children?

The Christian home is the Master's workshop where the processes of character molding are silently, lovingly, faithfully and successfully carried on.

–Richard Milnes

Read the statement by Richard Milnes. If you are a parent, do you have the sense that your home is the workshop of Christ and you are partnered with Him in developing your children? What about the home in which you were raised?

Parenthood is a wonderful privilege with an awesome responsibility. Parents are not to passively watch their children grow up. They are to "bring them up," which suggests active involvement in the process of providing, nurturing, training, and instructing. What is the difference between training and instructing? How does a parent provide the "training and instruction of the Lord"?

Meditate on Ephesians 6:5–9

Workers are to relate to their employers with obedience, respect, and sincerity. What is the motivation for obeying requests of an employer? What should Christians do if their employers ask them to do things considered inappropriate? What if they are not the kind of people who can be respected?

Christian workers are to do their work as if they were obeying Christ, as if they were slaves of Christ, and as if they were serving the Lord. Do you look at your work that way?

Read the statement by Charles Stelzle. How can you take the common tasks that you must do and make them "immortal tasks"?

God never calls a lazy, disgruntled man to a job which requires the finer qualities of real manhood. Every worker may make the commonest job an immortal task.

–Charles Stelzle

CONTEMPLATION ✦ REFLECT AND YIELD

How would your world be different if people around you genuinely cared about each other? How could you be more caring? Are you willing to remove relational barriers that may exist in your life?

PRAYER ✦ RESPOND TO GOD

People flourish when living and working within loving relationships. Who needs to experience an expression of your love? Pray and ask God to lead you to persons today with whom you can share the love of God.

INCARNATION ✝ LIVE THE WORD

We are to be like Christ in our relationships and work as if we are working for Him. Make a list of changes you would like to see in the atmosphere of your home and your work. Name something you can do today to help change this atmosphere.

LIVING VICTORIOUSLY IN A HOSTILE WORLD

Listening for God through Ephesians 6:10–24

SUMMARY

Believers enjoy grace that has been lavished on them, along with all of the accompanying blessings. They have been lifted up into the heavenly realms in Christ. The problem is that they must live their new life in a world where they experience adversity and attacks by ungodly powers.

Living victoriously requires the following: recognizing the enemy, taking a committed stand, relying on the strength of God, putting on the protective gear that is available, and praying. The great thing about these requirements is that each one comes directly from the hand of God.

Paul closes out this rich letter with thoughts about others. He could have talked about the difficulties he was facing in prison, but he simply asked for prayer that he would be fearless and effective in his witness. He wanted to finish well. A bit of heaven filled his cell and caused life in a hostile world to still be purposeful, endurable, and victorious. He wrote this section so the same could be true of you, regardless of what imprisons you or what adversity you may be facing.

SILENCE ✝ LISTEN FOR GOD

Speak the name of a person who needs God's presence and help today. Now listen as the Holy Spirit interprets to the Father the groaning of your heart for things you don't know enough about to pray effectively.

PREPARATION ✝ FOCUS YOUR THOUGHTS

For what do you most often pray for yourself? Do you pray as much for others as you do for yourself? If you could improve your prayer practices, what would you most like to change?

READING ✝ HEAR THE WORD

The cosmic war between good and evil—God and Satan—is sometimes found raging in our personal worlds. The battle may be fought internally or externally, with physical or spiritual adversaries, or with persons or circumstances. A common result of living in a fallen world is that we must deal with temptations, adversity, illnesses, trauma, relational conflict, doubts, and resistance to our commitments.

Here Paul identifies some of life's adversaries and the way to appropriate the power of God so you can be strong and stand. This isn't heaven. Bad things happen to you. But your relationship with Christ and His Spirit residing within you can help you overcome in the struggle.

Read Ephesians 6:10–24. Note how frequently the word *stand* occurs. Standing is portrayed as the posture of the person who is strong in the power of God.

MEDITATION ✝ ENGAGE THE WORD

Meditate on Ephesians 6:10–13

What sources of conflict does Paul identify? What do you understand these to be?

Paul indicates that our strength to overcome comes from God. How can you appropriate God's power in your life so you can be strong?

One of your adversaries is identified as the devil, who is scheming against you. Who is the devil? What attributes and powers does he possess? In what ways might he scheme against you?

God has made adequate provision for you to be able to stand against the schemes of the devil. What provision does He offer? What is your responsibility in being made adequate?

In the sidebar quote, Aaron Hill suggests that trials can have a valued effect in our lives. In what way? Do you agree with what he says?

> There is no merit where there is no trial; and until experience stamps the mark of strength, cowards may pass for heroes, and faith for falsehood.
>
> —Aaron Hill

Meditate on Ephesians 6:13–17

Reflect on how Paul uses the word *stand* and what he might mean by each use.

The armor of God is identified in these verses. What is the importance of each piece for a Christian's protection and powerful living? What must you do to put on each piece of armor?

Is there a particular piece of armor that has proven effective and meaningful in your experience? Is there a piece that may be missing in your armament?

In the sidebar John Greenleaf Whittier echoes Paul's insights about the believer's struggles. How do his words compare to your resolve?

So let it be in God's own might

We gird us for the coming fight,

And, strong in Him whose cause is ours

In conflict with unholy powers,

We grasp the weapons He has given,—

The Light and Truth, and Love of Heaven.

—John Greenleaf Whittier

Meditate on Ephesians 6:18–20

There were those who thought they could silence Paul and curtail his ministry by placing him in prison. Paul referred to himself as "an ambassador in chains." What did he mean by this?

Paul did not pray for freedom from prison, but rather for freedom to proclaim the gospel without fear. Do people more often pray for a resolution to their problem or for the ability to honor God and fulfill their purpose in spite of their problem?

As Fred Beck indicates in the sidebar, our power to stand is directly related to our reliance

> If you are swept off your feet, it's time to get on your knees.
>
> —Fred Beck

upon God. Prayer is a blessed privilege. It is also a critical necessity. How does Beck's challenge come into play in your own life circumstances?

We are strengthened by prayer—our prayers to God on our own behalf and the prayers of others on our behalf. What are you doing to cultivate both kinds of prayers?

Read the sidebar quote from Phillip Brooks. What is he suggesting about the focus of our prayers as we face the adversities of life? Can you see yourself praying in this way? Why or why not?

> O, do not pray for easy lives. Pray to be stronger men. Do not pray for tasks equal to your powers. Pray for powers equal to your tasks.
>
> —Phillips Brooks

Meditate on Ephesians 6:21–24

We are strengthened through the relationships we have that speak words of encouragement, faith, and love to us. Whom has God placed in your life that encourages you?

It is important that we be sensitive to the situations others are facing and be supportive of them. What means do you have of being made aware of the needs of others so you can encourage them and pray for them?

Paul's closing includes powerful words—*peace, love, faith,* and *grace*—that he speaks into the lives of these friends. Our words have the power to lift up or tear down. In what ways do you cultivate the practice of speaking words into the lives of people near you? Do your words uplift these people? Into whose life has He called you to speak encouragement?

Robert Hawker's benedictory prayer in the sidebar is a fitting way to conclude the study of Ephesians. It reflects the spirit of Paul as he closes his letter to

> Lord, dismiss us
> with thy blessing,
>
> Hope, and comfort
> from above;
>
> Let us each, thy peace
> possessing,
>
> Triumph in redeeming love.
> —Robert Hawker

believers who live in a world that can be hostile, but whose life in Christ and in the church helps them be victorious. How can you see yourself, with God's strength, triumphing in redeeming love?

CONTEMPLATION ✝ REFLECT AND YIELD

How could you more effectively incorporate a pattern of spiritual discipline in your life of prayer, Bible reading, worship, quietness, meditation, and witness? Are you willing to do the things that will make you stronger and more able to live victoriously?

Oratio PRAYER ✝ RESPOND TO GOD

Tell God about a situation in your life that has become a battlefield. Allow His Spirit to calm your spirit, bring peace to your mind, and reveal the means for living in His power and protection.

Incarnatio INCARNATION ✝ LIVE THE WORD

God wants you to be strong in the face of hostile influences in the world. List two areas of your life where you could be most susceptible to temptation. Name at least one thing you are going to begin doing today that will keep you strong when experiencing temptation.

LECTIO DIVINA

Lectio Divina, *Latin for* Divine Reading, *is a series of Bible studies that calls Christians to "listen to the text," reading Scripture as a means of hearing from God. The series takes its title from an ancient Christian tradition, one used and adapted by John Wesley, that incorporates silence, reading, meditation and prayer in Bible study.*

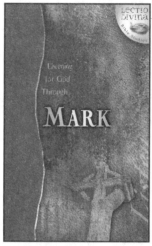

0-89827-301-3

Listening to God through Mark

How much can you sacrifice in preparation for eternity with Christ? Are you willing to give away money and possessions? What about control of your life? When He calls, we must be prepared to follow without question. Prepare yourself for life with Him now.

$7.99 each

Listening to God through Hebrews

Our society is filled with suspicion and cynicism, which restricts the intimate fellowship that God wants for us. By paying close attention to the character of Jesus, we can begin to experience the intimate relationship with God we were intended to enjoy.

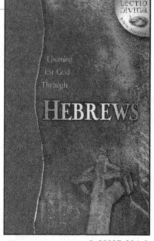

0-89827-304-8

**Order now for your small group,
Sunday school, or for personal study!**
Available from your local Christian bookstore.

Listening for God through His Word . . .

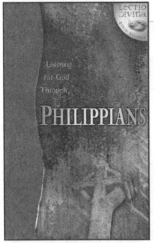

0-89827-303-X

Listening to God through Philippians

If you've ever felt isolated in your walk with God, rest assured that you share the road with many sisters and brothers. Paul understood that we each belong to a team that offers support and encouragement. Just as in Paul's experience, we both share the victories and the burdens.

Listening to God through John

How long could you survive without hearing God's voice? The people of Israel endured 400 years of silence from God while they awaited their Messiah. When Jesus came, many missed His significance to their lives. Many still miss it and Him today. Do you? Do those around you?

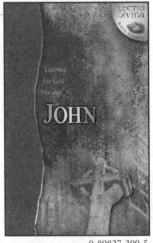

0-89827-300-5

Additional Studies in the Lectio Divina Series

- Ephesians
- James
- Revelation
- Timothy/Titus
- I Corinthians
- I & II Peter
- Acts
- Romans